I0876403

STEM AND THE HUMAN BODY

EXOSKELETON

Tammy Gagne and
Blaine Wiseman

AV2
www.av2books.com

AV2

Step 1
Go to **www.av2books.com**

Step 2
Enter this unique code
UKTOB3LAT

Step 3
Explore your interactive eBook!

AV2 is optimized for use on any device

Your interactive eBook comes with...

Contents
Browse a live contents page to easily navigate through resources

Audio
Listen to sections of the book read aloud

Videos
Watch informative video clips

Weblinks
Gain additional information for research

Try This!
Complete activities and hands-on experiments

Key Words
Study vocabulary, and complete a matching word activity

Quizzes
Test your knowledge

Slideshows
View images and captions

This title is part of our AV2 digital subscription

1-Year K–5 Subscription
ISBN 978-1-7911-3320-7

Access hundreds of AV2 titles with our digital subscription.
Sign up for a FREE trial at **www.av2books.com/trial**

STEM
AND THE HUMAN BODY

EXOSKELETON

Contents

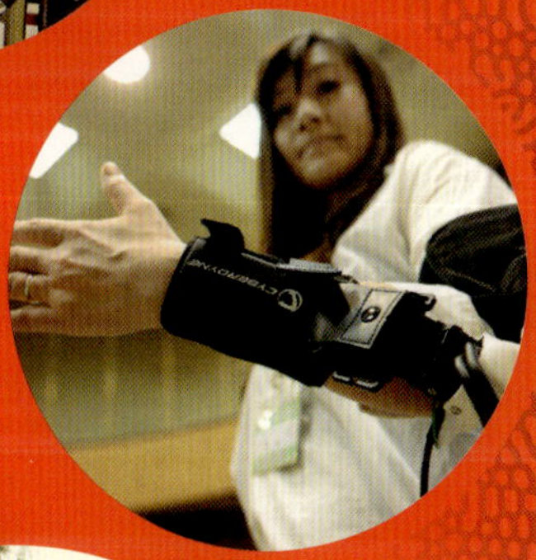

Spinal cord injuries are a major cause of paralysis. Each year, about **17,730 people** in the United States injure their spinal cords.

Vehicular accidents cause about **39 percent** of spinal injuries in the United States.

Roughly **300,000 people** in the United States live with spinal cord injuries.

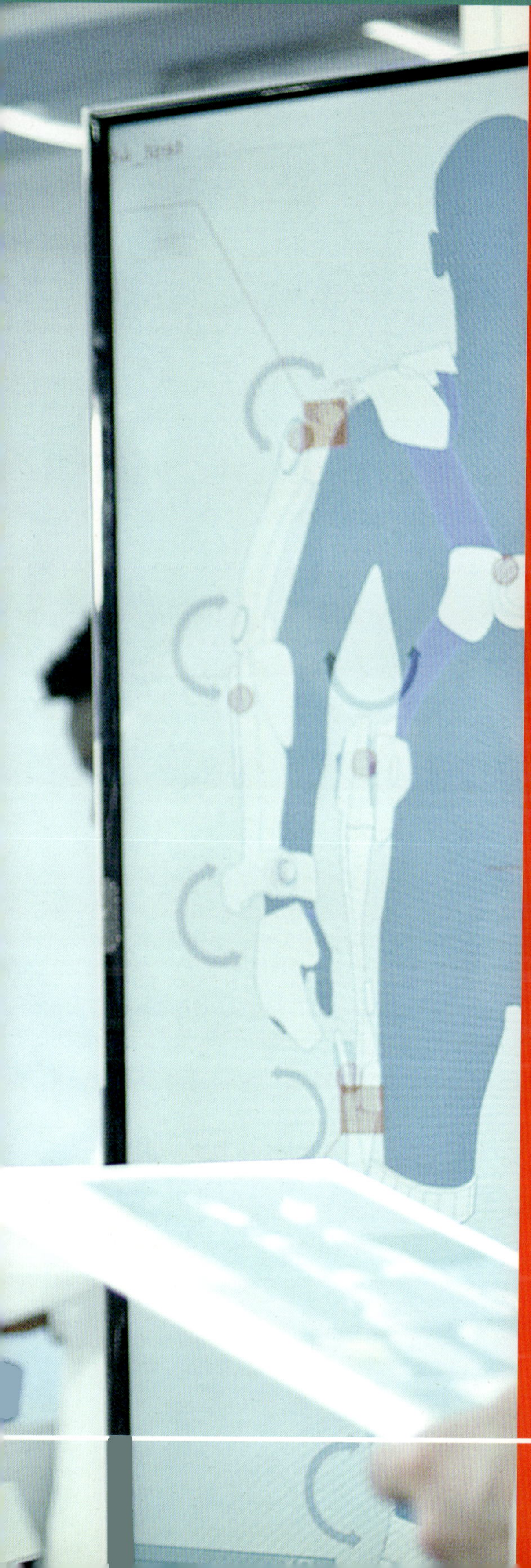

From Paralysis to Movement

In 2004, Steven Sanchez fell off his BMX bike. The accident **paralyzed** him instantly. Afterward, he used a wheelchair to get around. Today, Sanchez can walk again. He moves with the help of an exoskeleton.

This device is a machine that a person wears. The prefix *exo-* means "outside." So, an exoskeleton is a skeleton, but it goes outside the body. Different models have different uses.

The model Sanchez uses is called the Phoenix. He wears the metal frame over his lower body. He also holds crutches and presses buttons on the crutches. The buttons control motors attached to the frame. The motors move his legs.

Sanchez wears a backpack, too. Inside is a battery that powers the machine. Sanchez had to learn how to use the device, but in less than an hour, he could walk with slow, careful steps.

Sanchez was one of the first people to test the model. Today, other people can buy it. However, exoskeletons are very expensive. Although many companies are developing exoskeletons, the devices are not widely available yet. Companies hope these devices will help future users.

People who are paralyzed from the waist down can use wheelchairs to move around.

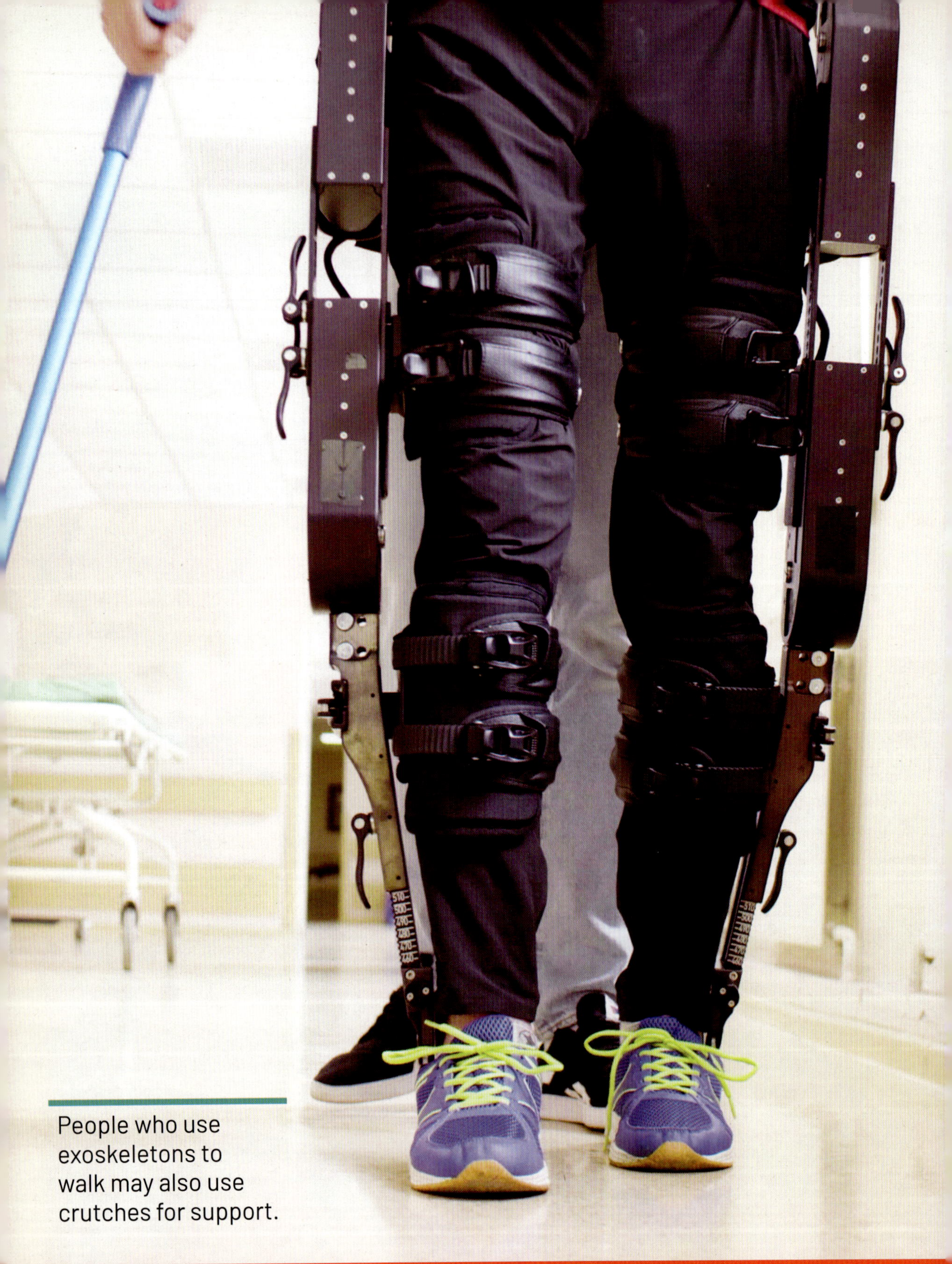

People who use exoskeletons to walk may also use crutches for support.

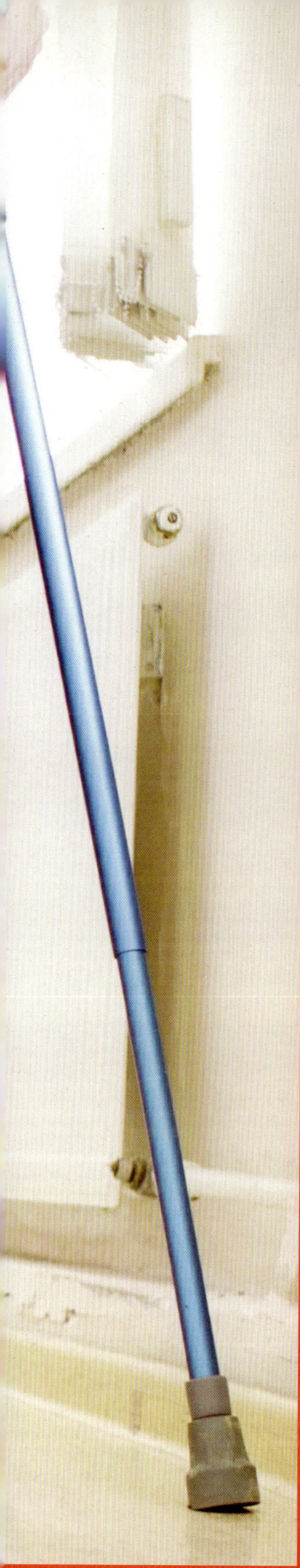

Some models are being designed to help people with disabilities. Exoskeletons could help users move their arms or legs. They could help users get exercise. The devices could also help users with daily tasks. Users could stand and take slow steps.

Other models are being designed to help **stroke** patients. After a stroke, patients might have trouble moving their arms. They may even become paralyzed. Exoskeletons could help some stroke patients regain movement in their arms.

Stronger and Faster

Certain jobs require heavy lifting. For these jobs, some workers can use exoskeletons. They can wear the devices and lift objects safely. Workers can lift objects for longer periods of time. Users are also able to get more work done in a day. A strong person might lift 200 pounds (91 kilograms) once or twice. Then, he or she needs to rest. With an exoskeleton, a person can lift this weight all day.

CHAPTER 2

Developing the Technology

Soldiers often have to carry heavy gear. The U.S. military thought exoskeletons could help. Soldiers hoped the devices would save time and energy.

Engineers built the first models in the 1960s. However, these early models were bulky and heavy. For example, one model weighed 1,500 pounds (680 kg).

Companies began designing their own models in the late 1960s. Many focused on helping people with paralysis.

Being paralyzed affects more than a person's body. It can affect a person's mental health, too. Many activities require standing or walking. Having to sit still all the time can lead to boredom. Not being able to move can also be upsetting. It can even cause **depression**.

People with paralysis often use wheelchairs to get around. The first models did not have motors. People moved the wheels with their hands. Today, motorized wheelchairs are often used, but even these come with problems. For instance, they create a height difference between the user and other people. Exoskeletons could solve this problem.

In the late 1990s, a Japanese company created a new model called HAL. This device helped paralyzed people stand. It moved their legs. By 2013, the company had created a full-body exoskeleton known as HAL 5. The whole device weighed only 22 pounds (10 kg).

People who are used to an active lifestyle may experience depression after becoming paralyzed.

Companies continue to develop exoskeleton technology. Some are focusing on **rehabilitation** devices. After an injury, some patients need physical therapy. It helps them regain the movement they had before the injury. Exoskeletons can be part of this therapy. They can help people exercise their limbs.

Reducing Pain

People with paralysis do not have a sense of touch in their paralyzed limbs, but many patients can still feel pain there. They often describe it as a burning feeling. Using an exoskeleton has been shown to reduce this common problem. Doctors believe the exoskeleton tricks the brain. The brain thinks that the limb is working normally.

Exoskeletons can help patients recover after a stroke or head injury.

HOW IT WORKS

Exoskeletons

An exoskeleton is a robotic frame. It fits over the user's body. When the frame moves, the person also moves, but the frame performs most of the work.

Many exoskeletons are made of metal. Others contain certain types of fabric. This material makes the exoskeleton more **flexible**. Some models even contain **sensors**. The sensors help the device respond to the user's movements.

In one system, a user leans on a pair of crutches. The user shifts his or her weight forward. The device senses that the user wants to take a step and moves accordingly. It lifts the user's leg and takes a step.

Exoskeletons require a power source. Creating long-lasting batteries is a challenge. Batteries must be lightweight. They also must be small enough to fit inside a backpack. Big batteries are not easy for users to carry around all day.

CHAPTER 3

The eLEGS exoskeleton weighs **45 pounds** (20 kg).

The HULC exoskeleton can help users move as fast as **10 miles per hour** (16 kilometers per hour).

The Phoenix exoskeleton costs **$40,000**, which is less than most other exoskeletons.

Exoskeletons Today

Many companies are developing and testing exoskeletons. Some models could help people who have medical conditions. The eLEGS device is one example. Users move the crutches. From this motion, the device senses how the user wants to move. The exoskeleton responds by moving.

Users must practice using an exoskeleton. It takes time to learn how to use the machine.

Other models can help people with lifting. For example, one company built an exoskeleton with a carbon fiber motor. This material is very lightweight. The entire model weighs only 13 pounds (6 kg), but it can help the user lift up to 33 pounds (15 kg). The model includes sensors. They detect when a person lifts or carries an object. The motor turns on only when it senses this activity.

Military models need to lift even more weight. The BLEEX model is fairly heavy, but it allows soldiers to carry more than 200 pounds (91 kg) in a backpack.

The HULC is another model used for carrying heavy loads. The HULC can carry the same amount of weight as the BLEEX. It works on any type of **terrain**. Carrying objects on hills is much harder than carrying objects on flat ground.

Exoskeletons are becoming more lightweight as the technology develops.

A person's gait changes as he or she gets older.

The HULC is also very strong and flexible. Users can crawl while wearing it. They can do other complex movements, too.

One challenge is work that requires **precision**. Picking up small objects is not easy for most robotic hands. Putting objects down in an exact location can also be difficult. However, one company claims its Guardian XO model has solved this problem. This model is just as strong as the others being made today, but it can perform highly precise tasks that most models cannot.

Designing a device that can walk is not an easy task. The machine must be able to **mimic** a human's gait. A gait is the way a person walks. It includes the speed and the length of each step. Even the way a person sets down his or her foot affects gait. Engineers design exoskeletons to copy these movements, but the result is still different from a natural gait.

INSTITUTE

CHAPTER 4

The Future of Exoskeletons

More people will use exoskeletons in the future. One company predicts that these devices will be part of everyday life by the mid-2030s. Cost will play a big role in this change. The machines will become more affordable over time.

As costs go down, more people will be able to use exoskeletons to walk again.

One day, governments may be able to give exoskeletons to emergency workers. Firefighters could use the devices to carry gear. EMTs and nurses could use them to move patients. Having the machines' help with lifting will make these jobs safer.

Making things safer is good for people. It is also good for the economy. When a worker gets hurt, the employer has to pay for medical treatment. Heavy lifting is one of the top causes of workplace injuries. U.S. businesses spend a combined $15 billion each year because of these injuries. Companies could invest in exoskeletons to lower this cost.

In the future, exoskeletons will be used more often in rehabilitation. Currently, most patients travel to medical offices for physical therapy. Patients with their own devices could do therapy at home instead. The use of the devices could also speed up recovery times.

Repetitive physical tasks can injure muscles. Some exoskeletons help workers perform repetitive tasks without injuring themselves.

FRAGILE

Exoskeletons are becoming more common in physical therapy and in the workplace.

Exoskeletons are not helpful without a power source. For this reason, engineers are searching for new energy sources. They are developing models that could run off hydrogen fuel. Future users might stop at hydrogen refueling stations to power up.

Exoskeletons could even be used for space exploration. Space suits are heavy. A suit that can move itself could be helpful. As the technology develops, researchers will find new uses for these devices. They will find new ways for exoskeletons to improve human life.

Mind-Controlled Devices

Mind control might sound like science fiction, but scientists are now developing exoskeletons with this feature. These models will receive signals from the user's brain. They will sense which way the user wants to move. It will take time before these models are ready for use, but experts are confident that one day these models will be available.

Test Your Knowledge

1
What does "exo" mean?

A: Outside

2
What is the name of the exoskeleton Steven Sanchez wears?

A: The Phoenix

3
During what decade were the first exoskeletons made?

A: The 1960s

4
What is the name of the exoskeleton model created in Japan in the 1990s?

A: HAL

5
How much does HAL 5 weigh?

A: 22 pounds (10 kg)

6
Why were the first exoskeletons built?

A: To help U.S. soldiers carry heavy gear

7
Can exoskeletons be used to reduce pain?

A: Yes

8
Does a person's gait remain the same as he or she gets older?

A: No

9
How much money do workplace injuries cost businesses each year in the United States?

A: $15 billion

10
What type of fuel could help exoskeletons work in the future?

A: Hydrogen fuel

Key Words

depression: a medical condition of deep, long-lasting sadness or loss of interest

flexible: easy to bend or change

mimic: to copy an appearance or behavior

paralyzed: caused part of the body to become incapable of movement

precision: the quality of being extremely precise and exact

rehabilitation: the process of restoring movement and other abilities following an injury

sensors: devices that detect things, such as movement

stroke: a disease that occurs when blood flow to an area of the brain is blocked

terrain: the physical features of an area of land

Index

Get the best of both worlds.

AV2 bridges the gap between print and digital.

The expandable resources toolbar enables quick access to content including **videos**, **audio**, **activities**, **weblinks**, **slideshows**, **quizzes**, and **key words**.

Animated videos make static images come alive.

Resource icons on each page help readers to further **explore key concepts**.

Published by AV2
276 5th Avenue, Suite 704 #917
New York, NY 10001
Website: www.av2books.com

Copyright ©2022 AV2
All rights reserved. No part of this publication may be reproduced, stored in a retrieval system, or transmitted in any form or by any means, electronic, mechanical, photocopying, recording, or otherwise, without the prior written permission of the publisher.

Library of Congress Control Number: 2020937053

ISBN 978-1-7911-2412-0 (hardcover)
ISBN 978-1-7911-2413-7 (softcover)
ISBN 978-1-7911-2414-4 (multi-user eBook)
ISBN 978-1-7911-2415-1 (single-user eBook)

Printed in Guangzhou, China
1 2 3 4 5 6 7 8 9 0 25 24 23 22 21

022021
101320

Art Director: Terry Paulhus Project Coordinator: Priyanka Das

Every reasonable effort has been made to trace ownership and to obtain permission to reprint copyright material. The publisher would be pleased to have any errors or omissions brought to its attention so that they may be corrected in subsequent printings.

The publisher acknowledges Alamy, Getty Images, iStock, and Shutterstock as its primary image suppliers for this title.

First published by Focus Readers in 2020.

View new titles and product videos at www.av2books.com